I0813074

Fred Bock

Piano Favorites for Easter

Including Palm Sunday and Holy Week

CONTENTS

Compilation ©Copyright 1998 by Fred Bock Music Company. All rights reserved. Made in U.S.A.

Fred Bock Music Company

Because He Lives

William J. Gaither
Arranged by Fred Bock

©Copyright 1971 by Gaither Music Co.(ASCAP). All rights reserved. Used by permission.

f
f
1.
2.
mp
p
l.h.
f
ff
Ped.
a tempo
8va
8va
8ba
8ba
ff
Ped.
Ped.

Lift High the Cross

Sydney H. Nicholson
Arranged by Fred Bock

Majestically, with great strength

©Copyright 1974 and this arr. ©Copyright 1991 by Hope Publishing Co., Carol Stream, IL 60188.
All rights reserved. Used by permission.

f
r.h.
l.h.
f
f
ff
rit.
ff
ten.
ten.

The Easter Song

Anne Herring
Arranged by Fred Bock

©Copyright 1974 and arr. ©1982 by Latter Rain Music, (administered by EMI Christian Music Publishing).
All rights reserved. Used by Permission.

ff

ff
f
8va (both hands)
accelerando
ff

The Old Rugged Cross

George Bennard
Arranged by Fred Bock

©Copyright 1982 by Fred Bock Music Company. All rights reserved.

lightly rhythmic
mp
mf
stronger
f
ten.
mp
8va
1.
2.
p

God So Loved the World

John Stainer
Arranged by Fred Bock

Warmly (♩ =±86)

©Copyright 1984, 1996 by Fred Bock Music Company. All rights reserved.

mp
mp

rit.
f

p
ten.
ten.
pp

Were You There?

Spiritual
Arranged by Fred Bock

©Copyright 1961, renewed 1989 by Fred Bock Music Company. All rights reserved.

ten.
mp
Melody
mf
Melody
f
mf
mp
p
mp
ten.
3
3

Jubilantly
8va
3

When I Survey the Wondrous Cross

Based on Gregorian Chant
Arranged by Fred Bock

Moderato, with feeling

©Copyright 1991 by Fred Bock Music Company. All rights reserved.

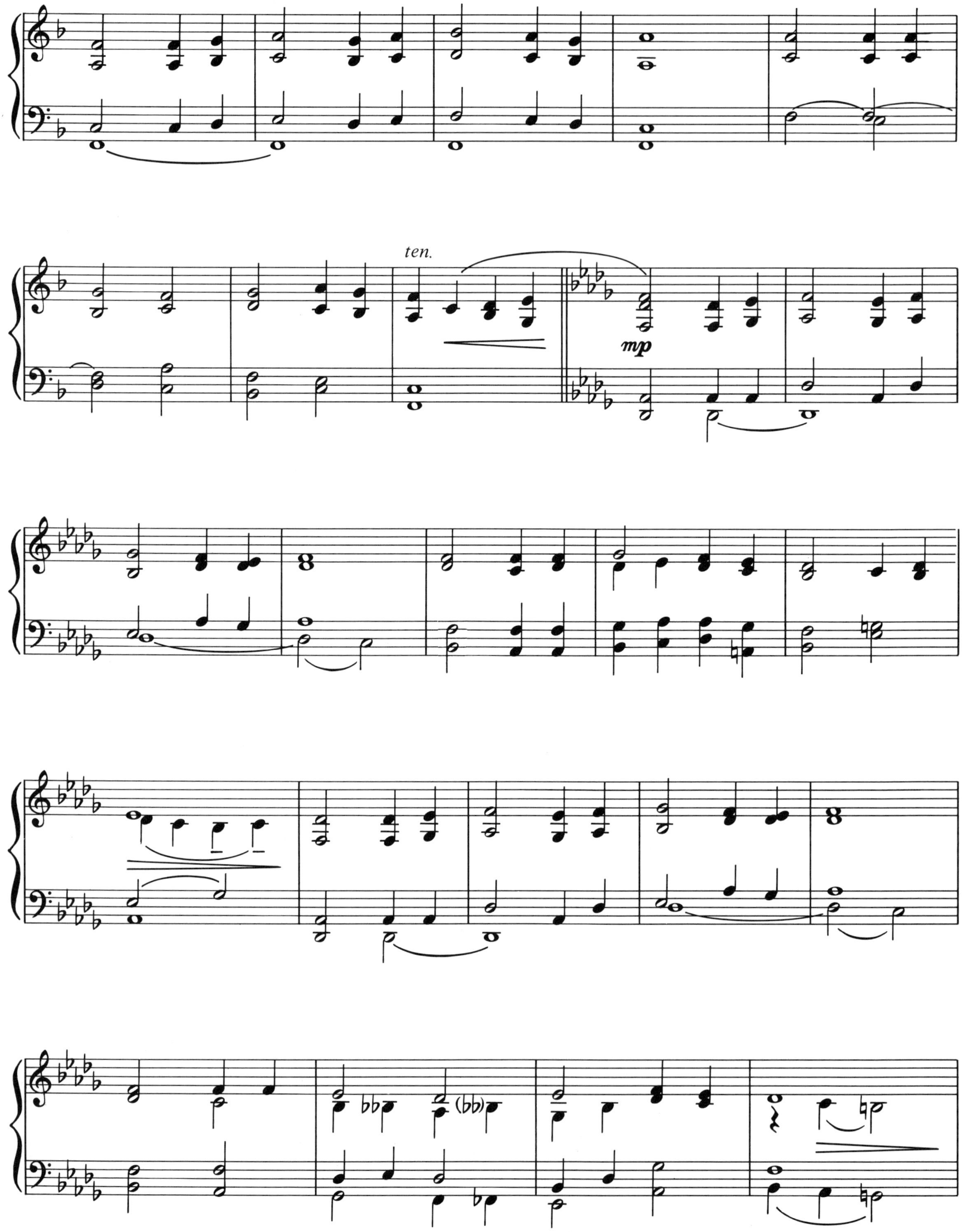
ten.
mp
(♭♭)

mf
p subito
melody
pp

All Hail, King Jesus

Dave Moody
Arranged by Fred Bock

Majestically (♩ = 80)

©Copyright 1981 by Glory Alleluia Music, (administered by Tempo Music Publications, Inc.)
All rights reserved. Used by permission

f
f
mf
3
3
melody legato
ten.
f

allargando
ff
slight accellerando
f
ff broaden
ff
grandioso
l.h.
r.h.
both hands 8va
fff

He Is Exalted

Twila Paris

Arranged by Fred Bock

With exuberance and rhythmic drive

©Copyright 1985, 1993 by Mountain Spring Music and Straightway Music, (administered by EMI Christian Music Publishing). All rights reserved. Used by permission.

1.
2.
mf
mf

8va (both hands)
8va

We Shall Behold Him

Dottie Rambo
Arranged by Fred Bock

©Copyright 1980 by John T. Benson Publishing Company (ASCAP).
All rights reserved. Used by permission of Benson Music Group, Inc.

ten.
mp
p

accelerando
ff

broaden
f
8ba
gradual rit.
mf
broadly
f
ff
ten. ten.

Our God Reigns

Leonard E. Smith, Jr.
Arranged by Fred Bock

©Copyright 1974, 1978 by L. Smith/New Jerusalem Music, P.O. Box 225, Clarksboro, NJ 08020.
All rights reserved. Used by permission.

mf
f
r.h.
f

ff
ad lib.
l.h.
ff

I've Just Seen Jesus

Gloria Gaither
William J. Gaither
Danny Daniels
Arranged by Fred Bock

©Copyright 1984 and this arr. ©Copyright 1991 by Gaither Music Company, (administered by Gaither Copyright Management) and Ariose Music (administered by EMI Christian Music Publishing).
All rights reserved. Used by permission.

ten.
ten. ten. ten.
mf

f
mp
p
broaden
building
ten.
sub. p
ten.

mf deliberately
ff
a tempo
f
r.h.
l.h.
r.h.
r.h.

f
broaden
ff
8va
3
loco
rit.
ff
8ba

Fred Bock Music Company